A NOTE FROM A DYSTOPIAN DREAM

ARTHI THIRUPPATHI

XpressPublishing
An imprint of Notion Press

Old No. 38, New No. 6
McNichols Road, Chetpet
Chennai - 600 031

First Published by Notion Press 2019
Copyright © Arthi Thiruppathi 2019
All Rights Reserved.

ISBN 978-1-64650-447-3

This book has been published with all efforts taken to make the material error-free after the consent of the author. However, the author and the publisher do not assume and hereby disclaim any liability to any party for any loss, damage, or disruption caused by errors or omissions, whether such errors or omissions result from negligence, accident, or any other cause.

While every effort has been made to avoid any mistake or omission, this publication is being sold on the condition and understanding that neither the author nor the publishers or printers would be liable in any manner to any person by reason of any mistake or omission in this publication or for any action taken or omitted to be taken or advice rendered or accepted on the basis of this work. For any defect in printing or binding the publishers will be liable only to replace the defective copy by another copy of this work then available.

Contents

An Elegy To Society

1. Part I   3

Musings Of A Fragmented Heart

2. Part Ii   25

An Elegy To Society

1. The Nocturnal
2. Silhouettes, screams, and scars
3. Audience to Selfhood
4. Unwanted Adulthood
5. The White Canvas
6. The Prison
7. Uncensored
8. The Bottle
9. Sacrificed
10. Equilibrium
11. An Amnesiac on Anesthesia
12. Birdie
13. If
14. Ode to a heart of ingratitude and naïveté
15. Fumeless metro
16. Untitled Ambition
17. Denial of Fear
18. A Midnight Tale

1. Part I

The Nocturnal
As the big orange Eye dips down
Below, an aura of oblivion
Swallows Society's Standards.
Absence of conformity, the
Constitution
Dissolved in darkness' despairing
Wrath. The dead arise; the living die.
Paralysis of the above ground. The
Eye faltering, limbs conscious but
Hunger left ungratified. Meat left
Rotting.
Flesh still raw, still naked. The
Obscenity left too exposed –
Vulnerable.
Erecting tombstones for the
Pretence. Raw sweat and dried blood
A privilege for the tongue, feeding
On unadulterated lies.
Cigarettes lighting up the
Night skies. Unlicensed factory smoke
Feeding pockets like the parched
Lips of innocence, the hearts of love

Aren't

Silhouettes, screams and scars
A sliver of a chocolate
Stained the corner of her lips
As she laughed with all her heart
Looking at this man who held
The last traces of truth in this
Post-truth society.
It was only a silhouette, though
A little figment of a rampant mind
Lost in (imagi)nation – the fictional
Land that wasn't quite annexed yet
By the corrupting corners of a pure
White house.
She threw her hair back carelessly
Exposing her scars, cuts and bruises
Not afraid to hide from everyone
Who dug a knife into morality,
Into ethicality into
Sanity.

Audience to selfhood
Her tiny lids fluttered open,
Slowly becoming an audience

For the trees, the birds, the grass,
The seas, the land, the empire
Of a mighty man whose mighty name
Eluded the newborn babe
Who still thought all of life was
But a game.
A year passed from the decade-mark,
Her curious lids sprung open as she
Became a more mature audience,
As she became a witness of conflict,
A void of despair that called for panic
Her eyes were an innocent sponge
That soaked up the blood and hatred
That society endlessly leaked.
Her breath then kissed the skyline
Of a city whose lights were too foreign
And she was now audience to a
Spectacle of contemporary sin,
Her eyes fixated on the nicotine curtain
As a cold, rough voice of false love
Broke into her swollen heart,
Escaping with her virtue in tow.
A curtain of opioids veiling truth,
The battle cry of a conformist
Led her to war against her identity
She was just an audience in the dust
To the chaos and confusion of

Lethal lullabies in Loneliness' lair
Phantasms of yesterday's ambition
Haunting her amidst the ranks of the unknown.
As her shoulders drooped with the
Responsibilities of womanhood,
She adjusted the mesh upon her eyes,
Audience now to a monochrome film
Set in the dreary town of Purgatory,
A painful reminder that hope will
Always be lost, just like a capricious
Thing that some call identity.
She stood with the weight of half a life,
The markings of her balance blurred,
Yet knowing the needle barely moved,
She wished for a pith more satisfying.
Her eyes now audience to her own life:
Hours and days and weeks passing
Fluidly through her arthritic fingers
Into a deep chasm of torpor.

Unwanted Adulthood

And all of a sudden I'm
Someone else another person
I can't quite recognize
With the expectations of
An Adult.

Poised elegant sophisticated
Smart, of course
Responsible and mature with
An alleged control of
Myself and everything around
Me I can't understand.
Paint all over my face
Tutus and ballet shoes
With princess tiaras
Tilted not quite the
Right angle I don't
Remember taking
It all off.
I need a career they
Say and a life to go
With it and work they
Say work harder smarter
Longer they say and I
Can hear them just fine
But screaming doesn't translate
The tongue and dialect that
They use all the damn time.
Mismatched and unrhymed
I'm in a blizzard with
Nobody to find me and nothing
To take me to a place I once
Could have called home.

Get up grow up live up
To the expectations of
A place they call society
The thing that annexed my
Dreams of a faraway castle
Where I lived forever like a princess
In the arms of my Prince Charming.
He doesn't exist they
Say once again so I need
To be a big girl and stop
Searching for perfection
While making myself a
Perfect Woman.
But what if that isn't who
I want to be or who I think
I could be?
Life is a dictatorship and quite
Oddly enough you're never
The dictator of your own so
You rest assured that there is no
Tribunal or court waiting for your
Hearing or opinion because
A genocide of your dreams
Could never amount to anything
Not in this land of gold, diamonds and
Perfect rows of ego.

The White Canvas

The White Canvas speaks in its own language,
Obscured to the colours fading to grey,
Every point but on its own a vantage,
For beyond it was not where beauty lay.
The White Canvas was an expression of
Simplicity in itself, a preserved austerity.
Yet a loveliness too complex for the mundane;
The Masses seeking ecstasy in the vulgarity.
The White Canvas slowly saw a stain,
A drop of red, upon a surface so white;
A paradisiacal entity subjected to be slain.
And on the White Canvas, the red
Bled, slowly trickling
Down; the drops becoming a downpour,
And the downpour becoming a flood. I see
Purity lost. I think paradoxical.
The White Canvas, with its naïveté
Mocked, its splendour robbed, now
Posing for a dernier cri, unthinkably
Unbecoming. Lured into a ruse of
Palpable 'beauty'.
The White Canvas no longer
Holds its pristine beauty; an
Expression of White fading to a
Shocking mélange of a jarring collection

That wails shrieks screams and
Shouts of desperation…
yet
hurts to look at because it simply has
too much going for it.

The Prison
And all this unfamiliarity blinds me,
A stranger in my own home,
Gaped mouth and lonely I roam,
Memories slipping through my fingers.
Heaps and heaps of yesterday's collections,
The forgotten phantoms of delight,
Ancient favorites no longer a pretty sight;
I see only a worthless treasure.
Old Barbie dolls lie dead,
The absence of a child to play,
Juvenile desires left on a glass display,
Incarcerated by fading dreams.
Homesick and longing for a love,
Taunted by hopes once mine,
Ambition no more my valentine,
I stare into a mirror.
And nothing looks back at me.

Uncensored.

The big letters called out
As much as the small words
Printed on thick paper
Armor against applesauce
Seuss never made sense then
Except as a canvas for
My Crayola brilliance.
Their strokes became funny later,
A serif font replaced my alligators,
My caterpillars, my hat-wearing cats,
And the rainbows dissolved to
A pool of monochrome text
That cast a spell promising to
Erase my puerile soul.
I don't scribble black crayon
On the frightening images anymore
Because there are too many,
And not enough crayon to wipe
Away everything that scares me,
Instead I let it consume me whole,
Ideology sinking too deep inside of me.

The bottle

Like pressure in a bottle,
I lie motionless;

Still. Lifeless.
Because that's what I was.
I try to suppress it all,
They pump more nothingness
An experiment; see how much I can take,
And I smile at it all.
At a loss of discretion
I simply welcome everything,
All the pressure I take in,
Wishing I could break.
And then I explode.

Sacrificed

Soft angels of justice lying naked,
The embers burning still upon their feet,
Sacred ichor of truth drying quickly,
Rotting, in wait for Them to taste this meat.
War fields seized by Satanic prejudice,
Armies fueled by illicit dark gold,
A blanket of snow upon bloody rocks –
Unwritten pages leave tyranny untold.
A cloak of darkness upon innocence,
Wrinkles of experience scar rosy cheeks,
Bitter retrospect my unspoken foe,
The stench of putrid lies and false hope reeks.
Death's darkening cloak draped on my fingers,

Darker daemons of freedom possessing me,
Spirits of Choice, warlords' Karma hunting,
Slaying the monster, the devil they see –
Me.

Equilibrium

It gives me reason,
She said about the tear
That reflected her vacant soul
The words carrying beauty
From her fingers to paper.
But too much hurts,
She said about the pain
That consumed her crippled heart
The paper wistful for her
Tasteful serif strokes.
Something just right,
She wanted out of life
The tear dripping on a laugh,
But amalgamation of emotion
Isn't just right either.
But her broken heart didn't know
Happiness existed without pain
And greater suffering not always
Made for a greater peace
So, her Goldilocks forever searched.

An amnesiac on anesthesia
The needle inching closer
The hands unsteady
The sterility unflattering
The white no longer pure
The pain becoming sharper
The numbness overwhelming:
Oblivion.
Life's paradoxes all summed up here,
Down memory lane a trip I now fear,
For it's the unfamiliar that haunts me,
Voices never heard; light I couldn't see.
The gloves inching closer
The light unsteady
The smell unflattering
The skin no longer pure
The knife becoming sharper
The numbness overwhelming:
Oblivion.
Pieces of me lost to your yesterday,
Volition not a servant of my say,
Still waiting for what I have never known,
Finite delight as your heart turns to stone.
The end inching closer
The blade unsteady

The stitches unflattering
The mind no longer pure
The grit becoming sharper
The numbness overwhelming:
Oblivion.

birdie
caged bird sitting
colored by alternating
stripes of freedom and
captivity its plume
disappearing to the cold
metal that taunts her
endlessly.
with the rosy
glow of innocence
she flapped her
chained wings earnestly
until she realized
the futility of her
efforts.
she looked at
just the bars of
freedom wistfully
and walked
towards

it and realized
they didn't exist.
a pool formed
where her golden
feathers stood
now an expanse
of just
Red.

If

If this copper would turn to gold,
And this rose to a diamond,
My heart to a beating machine,
I could say I found love.
If this life was an algorithm,
A series of code to follow,
And rules were in black and white
I could say I lived how they wanted me to.
If charters defined the legitimacy of sentiment,
A constant commanding over conduct,
And persecution didn't provoke,
I could say I dictated over my faults.
If justice could determine righteousness,
And emotions weren't an XSM-73,
The mind still ruling over this heart,
I could say I was alive.

Ode to a heart of ingratitude and naïveté
The angel's wings too
Sharp, a blade tearing open
My heart, mercilessly scarring
Devilish tissue of painful
Innocence. Constellations blurred
With the stars' blinding light: a
Masquerade hiding an obscured
Despondency. The seas no longer
Are my dominion, for I cannot call
My unworldly self a sailor in
These tempestuous waters of
Misfortune and malady where
Vessels carrying dreams sink
Deep down below where
Naught shall be reclaimed
Even by my guardian angel who
No longer promises to watch over
These darkening skies.
the poison of their conceit and
vanity diluting the pureness
of my bloodstream
a body of flesh and love
giving way to a rich suit
of tubes and bones

*indistinguishable from
the corpses lying ecstatic
in the cemetery my angel
once warned me against
yet today helps populate.
where every inch of
air is stained by the pride
of the deceased and the
crunch of leaves beneath
your foot is the moaning
sigh of the few true lovers
and well-wishers you never
smiled at and never thought
back with gratitude.*

Untitled ambition
*And she sat.
Alone.
Desolate.
Pondering, wondering.
What the world was.
And she stood.
Barely.
Upright.
Whispering, trying.
To hold up the world.*

And she ran.
Quickly.
Insufficiently.
Faltering, breaking.
The fragile hopes.

Denial of Fear

She cowered under the pink sheets,
The Hello Kitty blanket that was refuge
From the monsters under the bed,
The ghosts haunting the closets –
All the imaginary creatures they denied,
Forcing her fears back inside of her.
The ghosts escaped her closet,
Creeping instead around her heart,
Its incarnation some painful love,
Love, disease and other disorders,
Her blanket was a tougher skin –
To keep away the deniers of her fears.
Expectations and toxicity took up
An intangible manifestation of hell,
The demons you could not see,
And therefore, did not exist in their
Choking version of a utopia whose
Borders were demarcated by the numbers
That oozed out from lifeless humans

In a green stack that was decorated by
Etches of portraits of Great Men who
Represented in these sheets everything
They did not stand for.
She did not fear so much the people
That worshipped this stack of notes,
As much as she feared the paper itself,
Threatening to consume all of Society.
The monsters seeped inside of her,
Money corrupting her soul just as she
Denied the very existence of it
She wasn't scared anymore because
Her fears consumed her.
And she denied their existence.

A Midnight Tale

The empty cups of cappuccino
Smirked back at me as the
Clock's hands ticked faster
Than mine desperately
Hurrying to deadlines that
The clock eloquently
Illustrated with its
Perfectly synced hands.
The eerie silence
Punctuated itself

Erratically with the
Heavy bombs in the
Distance;
Its error couldn't
Matter, though,
Certainly not so much
As the graphite stains
On rows of circular
Choices.

Musings of a Fragmented Heart

1. Absent
2. An Angel in Hell
3. Bitter
4. Elegy for our Love
5. Eternal
6. Hurt in Twilight
7. Incomplete answers
8. Mirage of Love
9. Not mine
10. Once upon a time
11. Perfect Imperfection
12. Reminder of Loneliness
13. Sacrificed
14. Satanic Wedding
15. Something I need
16. Stolen Stars
17. Toxic
18. Your Name
19. Uncertain Faith

2. Part II

Absent

The pages have yellowed,
The ink has blurred,
The cursive strokes smudged,
The spine ripped apart.
Your love still haunts her,
A diary of broken fragments
And the memories she still clutches
Etch upon a broken soul,
Perpetual reminders of who she is to be.
The warmth of your embrace eludes her,
As certainly as the comfort of your whispers,
This diary no longer soothes her;
A blunted needle probing a taut heart.
As you slip away from the realm
Of all that she knows, all that she loves,
She slips into oblivion,
Where she can forever be with you.
She wished on a star that didn't exist
For a dream that couldn't come true:
A lie that couldn't turn into a truth.
She felt the pain as perfection slipped away,
She searched the heavens for a word to say,

A constant in her unknown,
Wishing her heart was stone.
Unburied, lifeless her corpse was to lay
As her heart wandered in the fields of unreality,
Where wishes would stay wishes
And dreams will not become more
And lies will remain lies
And hurt will be subdued
And amnesia will dull the pain
And she would love a memory,
A perfect man who
Existed in but her dreams
A lifeless corpse she would never meet.

An Angel in Hell

An angel from heaven in Satan's lair,
Though entangled by the honey of prejudice,
Enticed by damsels, them young lads so fair.
To this contemporary inferno,
Sans fickle beauty no longer his own
An unspeakable descent to hell's lows.
The devils of pride pushing him away
Chasing after love so capricious
Whispered that beauty wasn't meant to stay.
But it was his odyssey, to his girl,
Escapade of impossibility,

Demons' path of misfortune to unfurl.
Alas! She no longer belonged to him,
A possession of forces unspoken
Heart stolen; gentle soul now something grim.
The incarnation of another force,
His love fell into a sepulchral spell,
Feeble remains to set his heart on course.
An absence of the knowledge of his loss,
Despondency without his girl ensued,
And the stars above taunted with their cross.
He searched the heavens for his stolen heart,
For that was where he thought her to reside,
Loyalty still being his mastered art.
And her body lay upon a deathbed,
The seventh circle of hell's prisoner,
And broken orifices of love bled.
He wandered into hell's enticing gate,
Never once believing he'd find her there,
Satan claimed another one tonight.
A distorted corpse his eyes caught sight of
Showed him the falsity of their old love
A broken dream, emotions getting tough,
Her weakening body reaching to him,
A single touch relieving him of pain:
Amnesia. Her fingers became the poison of Lethe.

Bitter

An abyss of pain I don't understand,
Success now somehow a contraband,
It's still an idea that rings unfamiliarity
As it all fades to nothingness in my head.
Navigating beyond a darkening gate
My sinking ship a vessel from fate,
And how I wish I could become captain
Not of these seas but of my soul at least.
Your words of cold logic penetrate me,
Hurt, just as my own once guaranteed
To those I may have slaughtered before,
Apologetic, I'll fall to my bruised knees.
For you've shown me the pain of letters
A force that love cannot ever deter,
I'll stand now with my head bowed down
And accept my defeat with grace.

Elegy for our love

A promise of infiniteness,
A tale of forever,
All the things I thought would last
Now cackling, my smiles vanishing fast.
I want to break all these clocks,
Ticking to the fading echoes of my
Heartbeat. The hour's minutes

Turn to an absence of absolutes.
Wading through a limbo of memory,
I see happiness weaved to a myth.
Yet, eluding me are the words to deny
Our oeuvre turning to a lie.
Sequestered I see it, decaying slowly
A hue of black upon that amber, the
Beauty bids its adieu,
A sepulchral spell coming in lieu.
Irreparable, as certain as death,
I hold our lifeless remains, as
The cremated soul drifts far away,
Where our blinded eyes won't lay.

Eternal

Lackluster conversation invading
A once exciting love,
Promises of forever not so
More inciting an adrenaline rush
Trudging through tempestuous taciturnity.
Adrenaline escaping taut arteries,
Cracked lips evading kisses and smiles
Painful obligation forcing declarations
Of a love still ancient yet undefined
Rusting rows of romance recalled.
Ecstasy now slipping into my oblivion

Lust no longer a propelling force
I ponder once again the meaning of
A love that you promised me that stayed
Unique, unfazed and usurping unhappiness.
Realizing the depth that lay beyond
Everything miniscule I longed for and
The incessant bawling of a tired teenager
Drinking in the veracity of your emotion,
Stopping the sin of superficiality.
I understand now, sweetheart,
The logic shadowing your every
Syllable and the incessant piloting
To do, make, speak and hold right
Tattooing truth not terrible temptation.

Hurt in Twilight

Just realizing the Sun can burn too,
Still dwelling in twilight's softer glare,
Need my lifeboat in this ocean of rue.
Shrouding that body behind night's façade,
Naked but for all that pain and the hurt,
Leaving behind a skeleton once awed.
Starry nights no longer my paradise,
Stuck in a dusk I can't ever escape,
Brighter light and some love that won't suffice.
Yearning for what I shall never have,

In yesterday's tomorrow I wander,
Broken by a love I never did crave.

Incomplete answers
Because there's a vacant space
Right there where truth once slept
And breathed and bred beauty,
Emptiness and the absence of echoes
Of what once took up the title of
Permanence inside of me,
Redacted stories spill in maimed
Syllables and foreign vernacular
In a voice that sounds nothing
Like the reassurance and comfort
That once belonged to a person
Who vowed to never let go
Yet stands in front of me today
Unseeing eyes piercing my
Disbelieving gaze of broken trust
Only thorns left on the roses
That evoked incessant laughs
At societal idiocracy and flaws
In the system we ridiculed but
Fell in love because of.

Mirage of love

Like perfection personified,
You look to me my saving grace,
My silver lining in this incessant storm,
Promises I know will be kept.
You've crafted us a perfect bubble,
Ignorant of the slipping sands of time,
A little Eden, right here in Purgatory;
You're the Virgil to my Dante.
Your pieces make up my puzzle,
Incomplete without each other,
We could stay forever this way,
Blissfully cast away.
Perhaps I could learn to love again,
Catch the light in the hopelessness,
My resurrecting stone,
You brought me back to life.

Not mine

All of the stars now out of my control,
Reins of the chariot of fate in another's hands,
Your serif strokes dissolving to the pages,
Memory but another phantasm.
Consciousness lost to a limbo,
Every cell submerged in the Lethe,
Fables of tragedy taunting me,

Words too scattered for comprehension.
Meaning lost to yellowing pages,
The constellations haphazard,
My compass needle pointing to only you,
Directions gone awry.

Once upon a time
The box of memories beckoned
Her over, a sealed box overflowing
And threatening to explode.
Her failing hands shook as the
Wrinkles caught the dim candlelight
Picking the lock on the box.
A baby asleep in the arms
Of a mother smiled back
At the old woman behind paper.
She slept now in the arms
Of another in a foreign place
Cursed of dangerous wanderlust.
A daughter peeked shyly
From behind the pleats of a
Woman's skirt in a playgroup circle.
She stood now encircled
By guns, hate and men,
Oblivious to familial comfort.
A ghost of a girl whose

Face holds more years than
She remembers haunts
Her today with the shadows
Of overdose and the
Bullet in the heart.

Perfect Imperfections
The Paradoxes cried to each other
"It'll never be perfect,"
Lips barely apart, eyes screwed shut,
Myths of perfection made up the
Air that forced them apart.
The Haters screamed to each other
"You're never perfect,"
Fists barely apart, eyes wide open,
Fierce aura of pride and ego
Took up the world around them.
The Narcissists cooed to each other
"I'm always perfect,"
Fingers of bling barely apart,
Self-absorption and a different love
Pulling lips downwards.
The Fearful whispered to each other
"Could we be perfect?"
And our voices rang sharply in my ear,
As realization dawned upon me that

Such a word could never exist,
Not in this dystopia.
Perfect imperfection.

Reminder of Loneliness

Taking in the warmth
Of an embrace;
The arms of
A cold night
Around my waist.
Kisses of a
Cloud lingering
Upon my lips
Not craving
For another.
Scars left
From the Sun's
Supposed love
Trail carelessly
Down my arms.
Pricks of a
Thorn leave
The rest of me
Hurting, bleeding
And helpless.

Sacrificed

Soft angels of justice lying naked,
The embers burning still upon their feet,
Sacred ichor of truth drying quickly,
Rotting, in wait for Them to taste this meat.
War fields seized by Satanic prejudice,
Armies fueled by illicit dark gold,
A blanket of snow upon bloody rocks –
Unwritten pages leave tyranny untold.
A cloak of darkness upon innocence,
Wrinkles of experience scar rosy cheeks,
Bitter retrospect my unspoken foe,
The stench of putrid lies and false hope reeks.
Death's darkening cloak draped on my fingers,
Darker daemons of freedom possessing me,
Spirits of Choice, warlords' Karma hunting,
Slaying the monster, the devil they see –
Me.

Satanic Wedding

And the voices of hate penetrate,
Breaking through my shield of love,
The devilish whispers of Pride
Marrying the demons of Ego.
The promises to avenge;

A façade of love created to hurt,
Revenge standing as ring bearer,
Trailing veils lifted by False Love.
Jealousy leading the shy bride,
Flowers of Prejudice lining the aisle,
Forces of my love falling weak,
Helplessness to break apart this union.
Matrimonial promises whispered,
The amalgamation of all I've fought against
Annexing my weakening soul,
My love too helpless to revive me.
My feeble protests lost in the chasms
Of yesterday's beauty and grace,
I fade away; my heart giving way
To the couple's home.

Something I need.
Reading your remains on repeat
Wishing I had more to hold on to
Like a pile of memories lost to a fire;
A single photograph not victim.
Every second a blur of something
That I don't have anymore;
Every day an uphill battle
Against emotion I can't control.
A dip into Acheron could be

Amongst my new ecstasies,
The now permanent lines of pain
Traversing down my body.
A state I must acquiesce to,
A circumstance needing acceptance,
This anesthesia fading, the amnesia
No longer my escape.

Stolen Stars

And all the stars in the universe
Disappeared without a trace
Leaving a darkening void,
A blanket luring evil.
The constellations fall apart,
Nothing to guide the sailors home,
The path to Neverland gone amiss;
Childish desires vanishing at once.
Twilight becoming a conch's call
For criminals the Sun imprisoned,
The lack of a rule of law,
An absence of the stars' defining control.
And then I looked into your eyes,
And a thousand stars shined bright
And I saw where the light will always be –
By your loving side.

Toxic

Cancerous feelings surfacing in me,
A growing tumor replacing the void
Of broken love, of destroyed beauty:
A dangerous experiment.
My moral compass gone awry
But the needle pointing to you,
I wade amidst the unknown,
Hoping fate will pull me through.
And the mind subverts the heart,
The command of a constant disintegrating,
I ponder the morals of life and love,
Of death and hate.
As the ecstasy of infliction fades,
All the hurt I've delivered resurfaces,
The scars turning to ugly gashes,
Bleeding effortless karma.

Your name

Its echo lost in the blizzard of the known,
Both syllables sounding foreign,
I lose the letters to unfamiliarity;
Another item upon the lists.
Its echo returns to me oh-so-sweetly,
Your baritone voice carrying it back,

The unpalatability bowing down to me,
Letters spelled out in strokes now tinted in pink.
Its echo thunders back forcefully,
Satan in your disguise won't let me see
The raw, naked syllables that belong to me,
Records destroyed by my devil's fiery wrath.
Its echo is amidst the melancholy,
A fading voice inks itself upon me,
I bow down to the might of the letters,
Memories only scarring me.
Its silent echo deafens me,
My stabbing voice of infidelity
Rings back a blackening void,
As I whisper a thousand times into the darkness –
Your name.

Uncertain Faith
The grey incense drifted between
Cracks on the door's hinge,
My hacking cough followed
A sharp ringing echoing
Through the home for
A summoning.
Anticipation of blessing
After the sacrifice proudly
Yet humbly presented

In a garb of "purity and innocence"
Weaved only in a length of
Silk and not in the heart.
They barred them from
Entry into the sacred house
Just as they were also
Barred once upon a time,
The holiness a proxy for
Exacting revenge from
A life that decayed a
Long time ago.
I sit in the back with
My legs crossed and
Eyes closed, seeing
All but the stone deities
That spill blood just
As effectively as their
Dusty M16; the only
Difference is that theirs
Is taboo and yours is
Sacred.
I used to cover beneath
The ends of your colourful
Silk sari, breathing quietly
So as to not disturb the
Tiny flame upon your lamp,
Scrunching my eyes and stare

Into the darkness under my lids
Searching for hours to find the
Blessings you ask for, to find
The face of the deities that
Give you the solicited comfort
That is your entire world,
Wishing I could understand
Like you do.
You guided my fingers
Through the consecrated
Land and the hallowed powder
As I stained my forehead red,
Frightened by the uncertainty
That you resolutely believed in.
Nine years later and I
Still understand little
About your faith and
I linger without a constant
For the absence of faith is
Not disbelief but rather
An overwhelming sense
Of doubt.
After all, I can only feel
Religion when I'm with
You.

CPSIA information can be obtained
at www.ICGtesting.com
Printed in the USA
LVHW030313190422
716592LV00007B/316